# HAMMER
# IS THE
# PRAYER

# HAMMER IS THE PRAYER

*Selected Poems*

## CHRISTIAN WIMAN

FARRAR, STRAUS AND GIROUX

NEW YORK

FARRAR, STRAUS AND GIROUX
175 Varick Street, New York 10014

Grateful acknowledgment is made for permission
to reprint the following previously published material:
Poems from *The Long Home* are copyright © 2007 by Christian Wiman.
Poems from *Hard Night* are copyright © 2005 by Christian Wiman. All are used by
permission of The Permissions Company, Inc., on behalf of Copper Canyon Press,
www.coppercanyonpress.org. All rights reserved.
Poems from *Stolen Air: The Selected Poems of Osip Mandelstam*, selected and
translated by Christian Wiman, copyright © 2012 by Christian Wiman,
are used by permission of HarperCollins Publishers.

THE LIBRARY OF CONGRESS HAS CATALOGED
THE HARDCOVER EDITION AS FOLLOWS:
Names: Wiman, Christian, 1966– author.
Title: Hammer is the prayer : selected poems / Christian Wiman.
Description: First edition. | New York : Farrar, Straus and Giroux, 2016
Identifiers: LCCN 2016019991 | ISBN 9780374167745 (cloth) | ISBN
    9780374715212 (ebook)
Subjects: | BISAC: POETRY / American / General. | Poetry / Inspirational
    & Religious.
Classification: LCC PS3573.I47843 A6 2016 | DDC 811/.54—dc23
LC record available at https://lccn.loc.gov/2016019991

*Designed by Gretchen Achilles*

www.fsgbooks.com
www.twitter.com/fsgbooks • www.facebook.com/fsgbooks

3 5 7 9 10 8 6 4

*For D.*

*I live to show his power, who once did bring*
*My joys to weep, and now my griefs to sing.*

—GEORGE HERBERT

# CONTENTS

FROM

# EVERY RIVEN THING

FROM

# STOLEN AIR

### Selected Poems of Osip Mandelstam

## MORE LIKE THE STARS

FROM

---

# THE
# LONG
# HOME

REVENANT

She loved the fevered air, the green delirium
in the leaves as a late wind whipped and quickened—
a storm cloud glut with color like a plum.
Nothing could keep her from the fields then,
from waiting braced alone in the breaking heat
while lightning flared and disappeared around her,
thunder rattling the windows. I remember
the stories I heard my relatives repeat
of how spirits spoke through her clearest words,
her sudden eloquent confusion, trapped eyes,
the storms she loved because they were not hers:
her white face under the unburdening skies
upturned to feel the burn that never came:
that furious insight and the end of pain.

# CLEARING

It was when I walked lost
in the burn and rust
of late October that I turned
near dusk toward the leaf-screened
light of a green clearing in the trees.
In the untracked and roadless open
I saw an intact but wide open house,
half-standing and half-lost
to unsuffered seasons of wind
and frost: warped tin and broken stone,
old wood combed by the incurious sun.
The broad wall to the stark north,
each caulked chink and the solid hearth
dark with all the unremembered fires
that in the long nights quietly died,
implied a life of bare solitude
and hardship, little to hold
and less to keep, aching days
and welcome sleep in the mind-clearing cold.
And yet the wide sky, the wildflowered ground
and the sound of the wind
in the burn and rust of late October
as the days shortened and the leaves turned
must have been heartening, too,
to one who walked out of the trees
into a green clearing that he knew.
If you could find this place,
or even for one moment feel

in the word-riddled remnants
of what I felt there
the mild but gathering air, see the leaves
that with one good blast would go,
you could believe
that standing in a late weave of light and shade
a man could suddenly want his life,
feel it blaze in him and mean,
as for a moment I believed,
before I walked on.

## ONE GOOD EYE

Lost in the lush flesh
of my crannied aunt,
I felt her smell
of glycerine, rosewater
and long enclosure
enclosing me,
and held my breath
until she'd clucked
and muttered me
to my reluctant
unmuttering uncle
within whose huge
and pudgy palm
my own small-boned hand
was gravely taken,
shaken, and released.
Sunday: sunlight
oozing through drawn blinds
of the dining room
over fried okra
and steaming greens,
cherry yum-yum
and candied yams,
Navy knives and forks,
placemats picturing
national parks.
*Bless these gifts*
*we're about to receive,*

my uncle mumbled
and my aunt amened,
before with slow clinks
and shakes, amphibious
slurps and gurgles,
they dug untasting
in, bits of gifts
not quite received
tumbling down
laminated canyons,
improbable waterfalls,
far, clear mountains.
Nothing stopped
unless I stopped:
their mouths surprised
wide on half-finished
mouthfuls, my aunt
in unfeigned alarm
straining a full bowl
or meat-laden plate
in front of me,
little jiggles
shooting through
wattled, weighted
arms and my iced tea.
Exhausted, sprawled
on vinyl recliners
in the dim glooms
of the half-lit den,
they shouted down
the loud television

telling me
which neighbor's name
was in the news
that week, whose heart
stopped in sleep,
or some man by cancer
eaten clean away.
*It's early yet*,
they'd sigh and say
if I sighed or said
anything at all
about leaving,
nodding their heads
at me and nodding
noisily off
like a parody
of people sleeping:
my aunt's face crazed
with whiskery twitches,
her glass eye slitted
eerily open;
the unmuscled melt
of my uncle,
broad-skulled, flaring
forested nostrils.
The lamp, handcrafted
out of Coke cans,
flickered erratically
if I moved. The clock,
shaped like the state—
El Paso nine,

Amarillo noon,
and the vast plastic
where we were—ticked
each itchy instant.
Then it was time:
my uncle blundering
above me, gasping
tobacco and last
enticements;
—while my aunt,
bleary, tears bright
in her one good eye,
fussed and wished
the day was longer,
kissed and sloshed
herself around me,
a long last hold
from which I held
myself back,
enduring each
hot, wet breath, each
laborious beat
of her heart, thinking
it would never end.

My grandson walks through walls he does not see.
Touching nothing, he touches tools and stalls,
A bucket and a clutch of warm eggs:
The torn-down henhouse, wellhouse and the barn.
He wonders where the fenceline was, the maize,
The garden and the yard; stands blinking back
The brightness under the unshadowing eaves
Of the house, even the shade tree sheared away,
High cotton blooming in these rooms of air.
My grandson, leaning over the white rows,
Over the long porch gone to light, picks
A lock of cotton and he wants to know
If I would live it all again . . .
                                        Wind stirs
In the leaves, in the windmill's vacant blades,
Spinning and spinning without sound. Wind threads
Unwhistling through the windsplit wood, over
The filled-in well where something of the cold
Stone walls, of buried air and clear water, rose
When children we called down to hear a sound
Survive us; and it stirs before it dies
These leaves that rise and fall like the leaves of the tall
Pecan tree in the shadow-flooded yard
When the day was done, the work done, right here,
Where killdeer cried into our silences
And locusts sang themselves out of their skins.

He waits, listening. It is all still now.

                                        *J.C.W. (1913–1995)*

FROM

———

# HARD
# NIGHT

## SWEET NOTHING

Built or torn away?
All I know is noise
of wood and workmen
woke me this morning
and for an hour or more
I've drowsed between
my body and next door
where a ladder scrapes
across the pavement,
tools clatter and whine,
*tick, tick* as someone climbs.
Time to get up.
Time to sit down
and try once more to work.
Time for Rebecca, the art
restorer from England,
with freckled cheeks
and fingers finer
than a watchmaker's,
who never sleeps
and lives on cigarettes, gin,
and Chinese food,
to stir upstairs, begin
the early ablutions
that have made these weeks
of fog and idle solitude
oddly intimate:
creak of bedsprings,

creak of hardwood,
stuck doors and drawers
and the rusty sound
of faucets coughing on,
water quicksilvering down
white shoulders and thighs
into the pipes around
me like a teasing dream
of rain; and the silence then
as she chooses what to wear:
the pale blouse
with its paler plunge,
the flaxen dress
that matches her hair;
*click, click* of her heels
over the floor, out the door,
up Clayton Street.

But not yet, not quite yet . . .
I close my eyes and let
myself recede again
into the pillows and sheets,
inflections and directives
in a language I can't place,
pink hues and pigments
of Rebecca's face
at my door last night
as she smiled, or tried to,
held out her fine-boned hand
the streetlight seemed

to shine through, and said,
"It's time we met."

The salt fog poured
off the water as we walked,
formed and tore
Sutro Tower, the bridge's
blinking girders
into the moldy keeps
and closes of Suffolk,
cathedraled Cambridge,
Rotterdam and Rome
and the huge high-ceilinged rooms
of the dream she'd had for years,
our footsteps echoing
through that empty opulence
of silence and chandeliers,
nothing on the walls,
nothing in the doorways
or in the long white halls
but the guards, gray,
impassive, motioning us on.

Up Parnassus, past
the hospital, where the Richmond
glittered between the park
and the farther darkness
of the bay, we came into the last
room of her dream,
immense, immaculate,

with guns of every kind
and time arranged
on the floor, all the gleam
and lovely grain
of barrel and stock,
trigger and hammer
hoarding the light,
as one by one the guards
with their sensible shoes
and saintlike patience,
their tired, proprietary
silence, pressed close,
waiting for her to choose
the proper moment
and means of dying.

It all runs together now,
her Catholic girls' school
and the famous cloud
she wiped away
with the wrong solvent;
the erstwhile fiancé
for whom she'd felt a long
elegiacal tenderness
in lieu of love
and John Constable,
of Suffolk, who thought
no ambition too high
for the plain stiles and stumps
of that place, no feeling
too intense or complex

for its mossed waterwheels
and random hayricks,
its mizzling, mortared sky.
"What in the world,"
an acolyte asked, "did you mix
these colors with?"
"Brains," Constable's reply.

How lovely her laughter,
unguarded, delighted,
as if her own mind
and what it contained
had surprised her,
as when, crossing Ninth,
linking her arm in mine,
from deep in the dream
she suddenly recited,
"Largo Star,
Long-barreled Luger,
Rast-Gasser revolver,
Parabellum Beretta,
American Savage."
And how subdued,
almost confused she became
in the moment just after,
her arm drawn back,
the guards near, circumspect,
and a feeling not of fear,
you wouldn't call it fear,
exactly, and not dread,
but merely a vague anxiety

for the form of things,
deportment, propriety,
a sense that there may be,
Christ, some art to this.
Does one, for instance,
shoot oneself in the head?
Blow open the heart?
Take between one's lips
the cold barrel in recompense
for all that's been said
or left unsaid?

"You ask a lot of questions,"
Rebecca said somewhere
out on the Avenues,
with a look I couldn't read.
I wish I'd dreamed of her.
I wish that moment
before we turned back,
when we stood wondering
how far we'd gone,
had, deep in the night,
in the steepest, most
possessive hour of sleep,
flowered for me,
accumulations of quiet
at the back of her neck,
the base of her spine
touched into such
fugitive and minor cries
that to have heard them

would have been a kind
of ephemeral faith,
sustained in the mind
only so long
as the bones and dunes
of her moved under
and over me in the sweet
fruition of loneliness,
loveliness, need.

But no. Burkina Faso,
that's what I dreamed of,
a border that was nothing
but a line in the sand,
acres of empty space
and fierce infernal heat
in which a man
with muttonchops and a waistcoat
wavered and stayed.
"So happy a death," he said,
spreading his arms wide,
"It was more like a translation."

Is that a real country?
Silence. Are they finished?
Or can they be on break
already, at this hour,
me still half-awake,
the fog still feeling
its boneless, soundless way
along my one window?

One does grow tired,
tired of pondering
some problem of balance
or proportion, wondering
what's next, what's safe
to touch; tired
of coming into rooms
rain has seeped through,
the walls awry, the floor
buckling upward; tired
of matching grain
to grain, seam to seam,
to make some one thing
that will not, one knows,
in time, remain.

How lovely it might be
merely to drift through the days
for a while, telling
the barklike body
and windy shiverings
of the tree moth from the tree,
attending to the sticky feel
of a bottlebrush bloom
or the way a traffic light
will change and change.
How nice one night
to go all the way
to the ocean and back,
fall asleep with the fog
distilled on skin and hair,

wake in the arms
of a not uncomely
English woman who says
"Really, though, a line here
or there, the color off by fifty years,
who fucking cares?"

Creakings, rendings,
the crash of some last something
coming finally down . . .

O Rebecca, wry Rebecca,
with your furtive interiority
and your English teeth,
your country Suffolk candor
and vaguely tubercular beauty,
you are not alone.
Always that man appears
in a corner of the dream
and, without hesitation,
without a word or tears,
makes of his face an abstraction
of blood, flesh, and bone.
As the chute opens
above you once more,
Rebecca, sucking him up
into the ceiling, laugh,
because what else can you do
when walls dissolve,
a floor widens to horizon,
and all the guards,

quacking like ducks,
take out their feather dusters
and tidy up the sky?

Don't move, Rebecca.
It's late, but there is still time.
As the fog disperses,
as the jokes and curses
come almost
into your consciousness,
and the hammer's makeshift
useful music
is briefly the dream
it ends, stay here
one moment more,
letting the morning's mild
explicit light explore
the curve of one calf,
little ridges of ribcage
and clavicle, declivities
of shoulder and throat;
all the lines
and all the little pores
of your face, the faint
capillarial glow
of your eyelids,
which slowly open now,
Rebecca, sweet Rebecca,
as I whisper in your ear
*Bougouriba, Kossi,*
*Yatenga, Seno, Bam.*

## DARKNESS STARTS

A shadow in the shape of a house
slides out of a house
and loses its shape on the lawn.

Trees seek each other
as the wind within them dies.

Darkness starts inside of things
but keeps on going when the things are gone.

Barefoot careless in the farthest parts of the yard
children become their cries.

## POŠTOLKA

(PRAGUE)

When I was learning words
and you were in the bath
there was a flurry of small birds
and in the aftermath

of all that panicked flight,
as if the red dusk willed
a concentration of its light:
a falcon on the sill.

It scanned the orchard's bowers,
then pane by pane it eyed
the stories facing ours
but never looked inside.

I called you in to see.
And when you steamed the room
and naked next to me
stood dripping, as a bloom

of blood formed in your cheek
and slowly seemed to melt,
I could almost speak
the love I almost felt.

*Wish for something*, you said.
A shiver pricked your spine.
The falcon turned its head
and locked its eyes on mine,

and for a long moment I'm still in
I wished and wished and wished
the moment would not end.
And just like that it vanished.

## THE FUNERAL

It happens in a freakish early spring,
some little nameless place well off the highway.
From where we're standing we can't be seen.
How we've come to be here's hard to say.
It's lovely, though, the handcarved coffin, the hole
beneath like a shadow standing its ground;
the flowers, formality, and not one soul
missing, as if this town were less a town
than an excuse for funerals; this mute crowd
with its out-of-fashion suits and useless shoes,
the solemnity with which each head is bowed
as one by one, and row by row, they lose
themselves to a keen indigenous grief
that binds them cry to cry and tear to tear,
until its binding is its own relief.
To hear their prayer would be to come too near.
We're glad for it, though, glad for the heaven they hold—
we know they hold—like light behind their eyes,
and by their consolation are consoled
if consolation's what this feeling is
of having something in us jolted awake
like children half-rousing in a fast, dark car,
hearing the tires drone, the dashboard shake,
until it doesn't matter where they are.
And lovely, too, the singing when it starts,
out-of-time, hopelessly out-of-tune,
yet strong, encompassing, as if it came from hearts
that knew as well as loss what loss would be soon—

a stab inside of every dawn at first,
then a scent, maybe, a story someone tells,
and each day a little less, a little more lost,
until finally some dusk they find themselves
standing like strangers at their own dead pain,
without confusion, though, without bitterness,
as if within remembrance itself they sang
that to forget is also to be blessed.
It's over. A whir of gears, a pulley's creak:
the coffin clunks awkwardly into the earth.
Now there's some final ritual thing they speak.
And though it's cost us time it seems well worth
the loss, as like a huge black flower they peel
away from this death so different from our own,
though we can't say exactly what we feel,
and though it's way too late to make it home.

# SCENES FROM A CHILDHOOD

**1.**

Untouchable, the storm-cellar door, its tin a pane of fire.
Long into the dark it's warm.

**2.**

Little things live in shapes the stones weep:
blind worms, grubs like thumbs, roly-polies
rolled up in their stonelike sleep.

**3.**

The ant an aimed light cripples into ash
is lifted by the luckier others,

borne down
the eyeless socket in the ground.

**4.**

Light wind pricks light across the dark tank.

An engine of insects hums in the cattails.

A sandhill crane stabs its shadow.

5.

What hand moves the clouds?
To what touch do they come so slowly apart?


6.

It does not end, the dirt and the distance and the seared air.
Stare and stare


and even crows become the light into which they fly,
that pulse of false water where the world becomes the sky.


7.

Is it painful, the locust leaving itself?
Is that what in the briar of night they sing?

How hard to the highest treelimbs,
to the toolshed and shut doors at dawn
their likenesses cling.

# HARD NIGHT

What words or harder gift
does the light require of me
carving from the dark
this difficult tree?

What place or farther peace
do I almost see
emerging from the night
and heart of me?

The sky whitens, goes on and on.
Fields wrinkle into rows
of cotton, go on and on.
Night like a fling of crows
disperses and is gone.

What song, what home,
what calm or one clarity
can I not quite come to,
never quite see:
this field, this sky, this tree.

## LIVING WILL

All afternoon in the afterlife
of little things that love,
or pain, or need could not let go of
I hunt for the will
that will let me let you go.

I am distracted and slow—
all the grainy faces
in old photographs, letters
from the dead, deeds to places
that are only air,

some bright nowhere
of broad fields and sunlight
that was my idea of heaven
one long afternoon
of clouds and steady rain

when you sat and explained
where a garden was, a well,
excited by it, the hell
ahead of you
just a brief tightness at your heart.

Outside in the yard, crickets start,
cry *here* and *here* and *here*,
night's thousand shadows growing tall.
And now I have it, formal, final.
I touch each keepsake like a wall.

*J.C.W. (1913–1995)*

## A FIELD IN SCURRY COUNTY

Late evening, cool, September, and the ground
giving its clays and contours to the sky.
The colors swirl and merge and fall back down
and for a moment, as the reds intensify,

I am a ghost of all I don't remember,
a grown man standing where a child once stood.
It is late evening. It is cool. September.
Pain like a breeze goes through me as if it could.

A town so flat a grave's a hill,
    A dusk the color of beer.
A row of schooldesks shadows fill,
    A row of houses near.

A courthouse spreading to its lawn,
    A bank clock's lingering heat.
A gleam of storefronts not quite gone,
    A courthouse in the street.

A different element, almost,
    A dry creek brimming black.
A light to lure the darkness close,
    A light to keep it back.

A time so still a heart's a sound,
    A moon the color of skin.
A pumpjack bowing to the ground,
    Again, again, again.

## THIS INWARDNESS, THIS ICE

This inwardness, this ice,
this wide boreal whiteness

into which he's come
with a crawling sort of care

for the sky's severer blue,
the edge on the air,

trusting his own lightness
and the feel as feeling goes;

this discipline, this glaze,
this cold opacity of days

begins to crack.
No marks, not one scar,

no sign of where they are,
these weaknesses rumoring through,

growing loud if he stays,
louder if he turns back.

Nothing to do but move.
Nowhere to go but on,

to creep, and breathe, and learn
a blue beyond belief,

an air too sharp to pause,
this distance, this burn,

this element of flaws
that winces as it gives.

Nothing to do but live.
Nowhere to be but gone.

# BEING SERIOUS

## 1.

Serious smiles a lot.
At least that's what they say,
His Mum and Pop
Trying to be proud
As all the nurses gather round
To squint into the cloud
Of little Serious on the ultrasound.
*It's likely just the way he's bent,*
The head nurse finally thunders
Into the awe and argument
Swirling through the crowd
Where someone mutters half-aloud
*In all my years . . .*

Serious never hears.
Serious spins and spins
With his dumb dolphin grin
In the best bed there is,
Where there's no guilt and no sin,
No child more inner than this;
Nothing to will
And nothing to want,
No body you both are and haunt;
No drug of disappointment
Or feeling that there's never now
(Or do these seep in somehow?);
No suffering the world's idiocy

Like a saint its pains;
No traffic and no planes;
No debts, no taxes,
No phones and no faxes;
No rockslide of information
Called the Internet.

Serious isn't. Yet.

**2.**

Serious hears a sound.
Not unusual, in itself, nothing to be concerned about.
Here and there there's been a shout,
A song he seemed to be inside,
The weird whale-calls of her gas.
This, too, shall pass.

Then it comes again,
And with a far-off force
Which a shrink less serious than he
Will have him dream is a drain
That all his impurity
Is slowly drifting toward
(*Down*, Serious says, *down!*)
Beyond which he'll be clean,
Feel no pain . . .

Then the dark erupts in a rain
Of blood and muck
He seems to mostly be,
Holding on for all he's worth,
Which isn't much, finally,
Little wizened thing
Plopping out to an earth
Where cries of agony
Dwindle to equivocal joy
(*It's, it's . . . is it a boy?*)
And some clear world lies
Just beyond the eyes
You can't quite open;

And everything is wet,
And loud, and broken;
And all of life is one huge tit
You're meant to somehow suck.

Serious staggers to his feet,
Slaps himself harder than the doctor did
And says, *I'm fucked.*

**3.**

Serious is learning silence
In the way most children learn to speak.
*Poshlust!*
He gasps after his first feeding,
*Götterdämmerung* in his first dusk,
His whole body writing with a kind of violence
As if the world had wounded him,
Words his bleeding.

*Anomie, Deus absconditus*
Drift into the air above his crib;
*Accursed progenitor, quintessence of dust*
Dribble with the pap onto his bib;
As day by day, and week by week,
Serious wrestles with this difficult gift,
Forgetting, which, it seems, he is on this earth to do.

*Boob, ass, oaf,*
Riving out of him like greatness going off;
*Ninny, crackpate, clunkhead, gorm,*
Leaving him gasping and bent;
*Fragments, sheep, rabble,*
All falling, falling from him
Backwards into babble . . .

Finally Serious lies there, spent,
Language like some immense ghostly mobile
Bobbing just above his bed,
All power of movement gone as well:

Useless little buglike arms, buglike little fingers,
This heavy, heavy head.

And now if there's something Serious can't quite taste,
Or if he feels too acutely his own waste,
Or knows too acutely what he can't tell,
He screams and screams
Until the world knows what Serious means.

**4.**

Serious goes to school.
*Just try it*, his Mum says
As she lets go his hand
And wipes a last glaze
Of doughnut from his nose,
And Serious, insofar as Serious can,
Does give it a good try,
Though it's hard to understand
Why they keep taking a break
From taking breaks, or why
They can't simply walk
In line down the hall,
Or what, finally, is at stake
In a game of kickball.

It's time to draw a tree.
What a relief to work alone,
Serious thinks, as he picks a scab
For just the right tinge of sky,
Breaks his sugar cookie
To make a place of stone,
And fashions out of bread
A man with a huge head
And huge, ruined wings,
Gasping at all the ruined things
To which he's tumbled.
And calls it: *Cookie, Crumbled.*

*Oh my*, the teacher says
When she walks by,

*Those are interesting trees.*
Serious closes his eyes and sees
As in a vision of doom
Himself drowning in schools,
A whole ocean of fools
Nipping, nipping at him
With their tiny, tiny teeth.
And Serious sighs
With a prophet's wisdom
As he climbs up into his seat,
Stares out across the room
And like a prophet cries:
*You're all going to die!*

The class is a tomb.
Serious, rigid, waits.
A girl in pigtails giggles,
Then another near the back.
And as if along a fuse
The giggling goes
Up and down the rows
Till someone makes a crack
About his coat and tie
And the laughter detonates.

Serious climbs slowly down
Into that inferno of sound
Which the teacher's shouts
Are only driving higher,
Packs up his lunchbox, his dignity,
And his copy of Sartre,

And strides with a prophet's gaze
Through all that derisive fire.
Only once does he turn,
Briefly, to look back through the blaze
At the iron fact of his art,
Smaller from here, but unburned.

**5.**

Serious loves his Mum.
And then he doesn't, quite.
It's that way with everything—
Baths and plums,
The blessèd silence of night.

*Would you like to help with this?*
His mother asks
As she rolls out biscuit dough
And cuts it with a glass
Or folds the clothes
Still warm from the sun.
But Serious knows
He was born with a task,
And though he touches the clothes
And tastes the dough,
Serious says, *No.*

Serious stays in the bath
Until his skin is shriveled and cold,
Eats himself sick on plums,
Feels in the dark
The dark he becomes,
And cries out in the night for his Mum.

**6.**

Serious is older now.
He just is.
*Thank God*, Serious says,
For whom childhood, that stupid carousel that never stops,
Always had an element of disingenuousness:
The tristesse of lollipops,
The sham of naps;
Fools dandling you on their laps
So you can play horsey, which damn sure isn't serious;
And all that endless business
Of pretending to be curious
About the most obvious things:
What's night? Where's Mama-Cat?
What's wrong with Pop? Can God die?
Why, why, why?

To hell with that,
Serious thinks, as he sits incinerating memories
One by one,
Saying their names as he feeds them
Like photographs to a fire:
Here he is in a baseball uniform
Squinting back the sun;
Here in a blue tuxedo with a ruffled front;
And here, Lord, with pimples.
He pauses a moment.
Do memories *have* names?
And what, exactly, are these flames?
To hell with that!
Done.

Serious owns a car, pays taxes,
Contemplates a pension,
Has a crease of gray along his temples,
But he is young, young.
He develops headaches, begins sleeping badly, and relaxes,
You might say, into the constant tension
That he really always was,
With far, far too much to do
To look anywhere but onward,
Or to answer the questions of a child
With anything true.

7.

Serious isn't Stupid,
Though they go to the same gym.
Serious sees him dropping weights
Or picking his butt and thinks,
At least I'm not him.
Nor is he Mean or Vain,
Those chiseled twins
With matching boots and belts,
Nor Smug who notes their sins,
Nor Shallow noting something else;
He isn't useless Timid
Who no matter what won't complain,
Nor fat-assed Nice sweating honey
On all the machines,
Nor Self-Loathing who smudges mirrors,
Nor Whacked who licks them clean.
Serious isn't Funny.

Serious spreads his towel on the bench,
Sits down in front of his own image,
And Serious strains at a serious weight.
And never, not once, when he's seen
In myriad mirrors around the room
That everyone else is straining too,
Has he caught himself too late
And finished with a roar
And more strength
Than he's ever had before:
*I AM NOT YOU!*

**8.**

Serious has a date with Doom.
It's not the first, and seems unlikely to be the last,
For they get on quite well, Doom and he,
Share similar pasts
And similar ideas about what life should be.
It seems, in fact, that this might just bloom.

And what a relief.
After Morose and Mad and Neurotic;
After almost falling for Grief,
Who was so exotic
She made all the others seem tame.
Then to discover she even lied about her name.
And to sleep with another Serious! *That* was odd,
Like wrestling with an angel,
Though it was hard to tell from that rough unsated tangle
Which one was Serious, and which one God.

But how easy it is to be himself with Doom,
Serious thinks, as he puts the wine in to chill
And sets two glasses on a tray,
Who always wants whatever Serious wants
And always agrees with what he has to say;
Who doesn't need to hear that whole spiel
About "going too fast" or "needing more room";
And who doesn't probe and pry that long needle into his brain
—*What do you feel? What do you feel?*—
Until it's all Serious can do not to stand up and scream: *Pain!*

Lucky to be alive.
And if he still has no clear idea where she lives,
And never knows quite when she'll arrive,
Still, something about Doom feels right
To Serious, and he looks forward to their dates.
He checks himself in the mirror, dims the light,
And waits.

**9.**

Serious is a traveler.
"Traveling broadens the mind,"
The man beside him says,
His tray table down and seat reclined
Even as they're taking off,
And Serious, who has his eyes closed
So he can do what Serious does,
Begins to cough.

> *What do they say, what do they fear,*
> *Is this song joy or grief?*
> *This is a man, this is a god.*
> *Who are you and why are you here?*
> *To leave, to leave.*

The meal is over,
Which Serious declined.
In the shell-roar of the cabin
He eases somewhat, is surprised to find
He could almost drift away.
"What line of work are you in?"
He hears the man beside him say,
And Serious begins coughing wildly again.

> *What is that smell, what was that sound,*
> *Isn't that ice on the wings?*
> *This is the air, there is the water,*
> *But what do you do on the way down?*
> *You scream, you scream.*

How far they must have gone by now,
That old familiar world miles behind.
The man eats an orange,
And now he eats the rind.
He eats his plate, his plastic fork, chews
With animal relish his Styrofoam cup,
Leans over to eat bittersweet Serious too,
Who startles and wakes up.

> *Look at the desert, look at the green,*
> *Is there an end to that ice?*
> *Here is a place, and here is a place,*
> *But what is the space between?*
> *It's life, it's life.*

**10.**

Serious is married.

What a weird wind this is,

He thinks, so still at times,

Then stinging the eyes to tears.

And how he seems both more and less

Himself, and how it seems at once all of loneliness

And something he can hold.

Or is it he who's being carried?

He shivers, and reaches out for her again.

Or is it she who reaches, she who's cold?

What is this wind?

Where are these years?

II.
Serious experiences loss.
Just like that.
Flat.
Serious experiences loss,

As if he'd come to some sheer cliff
There was no way around,
No way to cross,
And found,
On the other side
Of a deep canyon, himself,
Experiencing loss.

Serious, when the man is gone,
Tells himself that he tried,
Tells himself that he cried and cried
For all he was worth
To the man sitting on the other side
Experiencing loss,
Who one day simply vanished, or moved on,
Or slipped off the edge of the earth
And died.

12.
Serious doesn't speak French.
This embarrasses Serious,
Because insofar as he lives anywhere,
Serious lives in Paris.

He feels the city stare,
Feels himself sweat, and shake, as he tries to wrench
The little that he's gleaned
Into the lot that he desires;
Feels shopkeepers look at him as if he were a liar,
Waiters as if he were unclean;

And feels, in truth, not at all serious,
As if he had a huge balloon for a head
And helium squeaks for a voice,
As if gravity could be merely a choice
He were making, and he might instead
Simply stop, let go, and drift away.

Finally Serious, opposed to epiphanies,
Has one he can't resist.
He *is* Serious, and to be Serious
Is to know something utterly or not at all,
And to know, moreover,
That as you let your half-knowledge fall
From you, *it does not exist.*

Just like that Serious is himself again,
Saying weighty things
About the flowers in the stalls,

Pondering a splendid mirage
Called the Seine.

And if he wakes saying *fromage*,
Or in some shop feels
Right on the verge of translating *please*,
Serious knows it's a dream,
And knows from childhood what to do.
Point and scream
Until the damn fools give you cheese.

## 13.

Serious has some culture.
He knows some things.
And if, as he begins to speak,
He should feel the immense wings
Of ignorance shadowing him, that dirty vulture
That squawks in drawl and drips tobacco juice,
Serious knows what shelter to seek.

Pick a name and Bach is better.
Modernism was powerful but diffuse.
Life's drained out of pictures since the Renaissance.
Technique! Technique! Technique!
And about all that spastic flatulence
Called contemporary art,
Well, Serious hardly knows where to start.

Serious sits through opera without a yawn,
Chews up books on which weaker teeth would shatter;
He can tell you where one brushstroke lies,
List the reasons courtly love is gone,
Pluck the speck of subject matter
From Henry James.
Serious knows some things.

He thinks and thinks and thinks
Until his ignorance shrinks
To the tiniest of flies
Alighting somewhere in the Louvre.
Carefully, carefully, Serious creeps
With his massive swatter,
Saying, *Don't move. Don't move.*

**14.**

Serious believes in nothing.
It's a nice day, what should we do?
What are you thinking?
What's been bothering you?
What's that you're drinking?

Serious spreads the paper on his lap
To confirm what's new under the sun,
Hears a *tap, tap, tap*
Against the windowpane.

*Nothing ventured, nothing gained,*
Floats up from childhood like a bit of ash,
And Serious, pausing, can almost see
His old preacher, that atom bomb of idiocy
Who every Sunday would explode.
Still, Serious thinks, there's a truth to set you free.
But who could survive the blast?

*Tap, tap, tap.*

Serious skims the sports pages,
Reads about a storm that rages
Far out at sea.
Some talking dog is taking office,
Some country wiping out monuments, expunging its past.

*Tap, tap, tap.*

*Goddammit*, Serious says, midway through a war,
And thinks again of that old bore
Who talked and talked and talked
Until you felt your head loll and sway
Like some huge flower on a tiny stalk
That one good breeze would break;

And how you'd see him afterwards eating chicken fried steak,
Chicken fried man,
With a tiny transistor radio in his hand
So he could listen to the football game;
And how his face seethed and writhed with what seemed pain
If he saw you coming to his booth,
And he stared off as if some great truth
Were finally, finally coming clear in that chicken fried brain
And like a prophet he was going to stand up and shout—
Until what plopped innocuously out
Was your own name.

*Tap, tap, tap.*

Serious puts aside the news of the day
And walks to the only window there is.
But there's no wind, not even the grass stirs.
And anyway, there's no tree.
Serious shrugs and turns away.
Must just be me.

**15.**

Serious sees a child
In the playground across the street,
Sees his huge stupid head and huge stupid feet
As he tries to keep up with the games,
And hears his sonar screams
Of delight amid the other children's screams,
And hears his timid weeping when they call him names.

Serious sees the child standing apart sometimes
Driveling to himself in silly rhymes,
And sees him pretend to look intently at the sky
If Serious walks by,
Or sees him simply stop and stare.

Gradually Serious starts seeing the child everywhere,
In a store standing in an aisle,
In the subway while
Serious is trying to work on the way home,
Or laughing with his family in a restaurant
Where Serious eats alone.

Serious knows the truth.
This child wants something, his whole nature is want.
And it begins to be annoying,
This novice cringing, all the imbecilic and cloying
Tactics of being cute,
The whole hangdog way he has of panhandling pity
With his freckles and his missing tooth,
Sitting all fidgety in his Sunday suit
Or babbling happily as he's leaking snot;

And then the air he suddenly puts on of being serious
When it's so obvious he's not.

Serious sees the child in the playground
Standing to the side,
Sees his face whiten and his eyes go wide
As Serious crosses the street and strides
Until his shadow swallows the child
And leans down close enough for them to kiss.
*I don't have time for this,*
Serious says,
*I've got too much to do.*

And the child says, *Who are you?*

16.

Serious kills himself.
*No, no,*
Shivering out of a dream,
Starlight and the hard glitter
Under the bridge's beam,
Serious, Serious,
Don't go.

Serious crawls out of bed,
Feels the cold in the floor
And thinks, suddenly, of lovely Mad
(Where can she be?)
Who'd bolt out of sleep and scream
*Farmers get up at four!*
It's three.

Serious makes himself a cup of coffee,
Which he doesn't drink;
Tries and fails to read,
Tries and fails to think.
Serious sits, and holds himself still,
Minute by minute;
Until the dawn finally comes
And he is in it.

**17.**

Serious lives alone.
It's better this way, he tells himself,
As he takes a pan from the pan shelf,
A spatula from the spatula drawer,
And fries two eggs the way *he* likes them:
Yolks of stone.

No more gnats of chatter over breakfast.
No more breakfast. It's noon.
No one prancing by with only panties on
When he's almost, almost broken through,
Or singsonging outside his door
*Serious, O Serious, where are you?*
No more!

But what, finally, *does* Serious do?
He sits, ignores the ringing phone,
Looks at a wall
On one of the last warm days of the year,
And settles back into the lifelong call
Of being serious,
Which is to see, within that whiteness,
Leaves being gently blown,
And to feel their colors as they fall.

18.

Serious gives a speech.
He sets his papers on the podium,
His glass within easy reach,
*Tap, tap, taps* the microphone.
How vast this venue is.
How absolute this darkness.

*To be serious is to be alone!*
Serious cries out with a triumphant look on his face,
Waiting for the echoes to end
Out there in all that space,
Which the words at once define and extend.
It takes a while, but they do die.
The spotlight lasers in.
He blinks hard, starts again.

*To know in every hand another's touch,*
*To hear a silence words only intensify,*
*To feel not too little but too much*
*This attenuated world—*

Serious begins to sweat,
Feels the back of his shirt grow wet;
Looks down to see his papers swirled
And scattered, the glass on the floor, broken.
What's with this fucking light, he thinks,
Or was it spoken?
He glares out at the dark, impassive crowd
And as if by force he could make them wake
Hears his voice growing loud:

Whatever you most treasure you will break,
Whatever you hold closest you will let go,
There is no place that you will not leave!
But to be serious—

                      Serious says,
Quietly now, because he has them, they are his—

To be serious, to be truly serious, is to know
That what you call your losses you cannot grieve,
For it was never quite these things that you wanted
—This treasure, this touch, this one place—
But by such life to be haunted.

Brilliant!
No notes, no flaws.
Serious stands back and waits for applause.
The hall is silent, utterly silent,
The heat tropic.

Serious looks around, confused,
Turns to the man who introduced him
Then can't remember being introduced;
And even given his credentials,
This suddenly seems a most unlikely topic.

Serious tries to get out of the light,
But the light goes where Serious goes.
He blunders to the edge of the stage,
A cliff
Breaking off into a dark
In which there's no movement, no voices, not one sigh.

Serious feels the rage
Draining out of him, and feels a chill, and whispers,
*Where am I?*

19.

Serious nears an end.
It's cold and getting colder,
And Serious, older,
Sits outside thinking of his good friend,
Who like so much of Serious is gone,
And thinking of that godforsaken dawn
After the one night of his life he spent outdoors.

*Tell me,*
His good friend said
When Serious staggered out to the fire,
*Which form would you say is higher,*
*Tragedy or comedy?*

And Serious, who had stumbled full-bladdered
In the night from a dream of bears,
Then dreamed himself the object
Of a dozen hungry stares,
Who had swiveled, pissed into the tent,
And sworn such things it would take a life to repent,
Serious, exhausted Serious,
Was silent.

*Because it's been troubling me,*
*Serious, that the answer can only be tragedy.*
*To be conscious is to be conscious of*
*Losing whatever it is that you most love,*
*And thus an art that's truly great*
*Will always have one deepest truth to tell,*
*Which is, my friend, this life is hell.*

Serious looks at the sky. It's late.
A small wind blows
The trees, and Serious, shivering, knows
He should head inside,
That he is not well.
But sitting here, letting his eyes close,
Serious can almost see that lake
Aflame with the early sun, and smell
The sweet burn of that wood,
And feel the way it seemed his heart would surely break
Were it not for the strange lightness in his head
As his friend smiled and said,
*But maybe earth is the heaven of the good.*

**20.**

Serious talks to God.
There's no one else left.
His mind is mash,
His world is ash,
And Serious occasionally forgets himself,
Though he is not, *not* Bereft,
That sniveling idiot two doors down
Who sits up late
With only ashes in the grate
And talks to God.

*See?* Serious says. *See?*
*Nothing.*
Serious spreads his arms magnanimously
As if to give God the floor.
God declines.
*Thou know'st the first time that we smell the air*
*We wawl and cry,*
Serious says, louder than before.
*And then we wawl and cry some more,*
*And then we die,*
*And then we rot!*
Again he waits in case
There's disagreement. There's not.

Serious scoffs, goes to brush his teeth,
Forgets briefly to avert his eye
From the mirror's glare
And finds his father there,

That gentle baffled man
Who, when there was no hope,
When he couldn't even stand,
Carved from a piece of soap
A silly yellow duck
And set it in a little yellow dish.
Serious feels a tingling in his hair
And mutters something close to a prayer,
*I wish, I wish . . .*

The lights go out.
*Goddammit,* Serious shouts
As he trips and falls
To his knees on the floor,
Banging his head on the door
As he tries to rise.
*GodDAMMIT!* Serious cries.

The lights come on.
His father's gone,
But there, at the edge of the sink,
Balances the little duck in the little dish
No serious person would ever keep.
Serious tries to think,
Steadies himself as if at some brink,
Decides he needs sleep,
That's what he needs,
Crawling fully clothed into his bed
And pulling the covers to his chin
Because, it seems, there's some strange wind

That's somehow gotten inside.
So unlike Serious,
To leave a door unclosed.

Yet here it is, gathering strength
As it blows his books
On the floor and it blows
Right through his body and it blows
Behind and below and above
And out of the whirlwind a voice cries

      *Love*

*What?* Serious says, as he tries
To sit upright and looks
Wildly around him,
Raising his fist in the air.
*The things . . . I have lost—*

Immediately he is tossed
Back against the wall
By the force of a storm
That has no source, no form,
And hears again the call
Out of nowhere:

      *Love*

*My God!* Serious screams,
Unable to help himself,
*What maundering politician,*

*What decerebrated pop star,*
*What stupid puling poet*
*Couldn't tell me that?*
Struggling to get out of bed
He starts to cough, then choke,
A riot in his heart,
A riot in his head
As he falls off the edge to the floor.
*Who do you think you are,*
He gasps. *Is this . . .*
*Is this some sort of JOKE?*

Suddenly the strange wind is quiet,
But no less strange the calm that comes after.

*I'm serious*, the voice says.

And Serious dies of laughter.

The dead man's famous.
No one now remembers him alive,
Or knows his name, or anything he did.
Still, a few stories survive
After all this while
Of a weird-looking man
With a weird-looking smile
That had, it's said,
Almost a kind of life to it,
Though the man was seriously dead.

And some remember how all the flies
Vanished for miles;
And some say no, no, but the buzzards had weird smiles
As if they knew something.
And some tell of an old woman
Who would come and whisper in the dead man's ear,
And smooth the dead man's hair,
And if the door opened, disappear.
There are even stories of that grim mortician
Who thought the smile undignified
And tugged and tugged so hard
He slipped and fell inside
Right on top of the dead man,
Whose lips, he swore, seemed to soften,
Seemed to somehow kiss.
And some remember this:
Before the lid was sealed on that coffin
And the nails driven,

There were on that face real tears.
And some say he smiled like a man forgiven.

The dead man never hears.
The dead man spins and spins
With his dumb dolphin grin
Through all the places where he is
When people talk of him again:
In classrooms or in planes,
In boredom or in pain;
In front of screens
Or in the spotlight's glare;
In days too mild to bear
And in the long nights where
The dark grows steep,
The wind wild,
And a mother rises from her sleep
To calm her serious child.

FROM

# EVERY
# RIVEN
# THING

## DUST DEVIL

Mystical hysterical amalgam of earth and wind
and mind

over and of
the much-loved

dust you go
through a field I know

by broken heart
for I have learned this art

of flourishing
vanishing

wherein to live
is to move

cohesion
illusion

wild untouchable toy
called by a boy

God's top
in a time when time stopped

## AFTER THE DIAGNOSIS

No remembering now
when the apple sapling was blown
almost out of the ground.
No telling how,
with all the other trees around,
it alone was struck.
It must have been luck,
he thought for years, so close
to the house it grew.
It must have been night.
Change is a thing one sleeps through
when young, and he was young.
If there was a weakness in the earth,
a give he went down on his knees
to find and feel the limits of,
there is no longer.
If there was one random blow from above
the way he's come to know
from years in this place,
the roots were stronger.
Whatever the case,
he has watched this tree survive
wind ripping at his roof for nights
on end, heats and blights
that left little else alive.
No remembering now . . .
A day's changes mean all to him
and all days come down

to one clear pane
through which he sees
among all the other trees
this leaning, clenched, unyielding one
that seems cast
in the form of a blast
that would have killed it,
as if something at the heart of things,
and with the heart of things,
had willed it.

## FIVE HOUSES DOWN

I loved his ten demented chickens
and the hell-eyed dog, the mailbox
shaped like a huge green gun.
I loved the eyesore opulence
of his five partial cars, the wonder-cluttered porch
with its oilspill plumage, tools
cauled in oil, the dark
clockwork of disassembled engines
christened Sweet Baby and benedicted Old Bitch;
and down the steps into the yard the explosion
of mismatched parts and black scraps
amid which, like a bad sapper cloaked
in luck, he would look up stunned,
patting the gut that slopped out of his undershirt
and saying, *Son,*
*you lookin' to make some scratch?*
All afternoon we'd pile the flatbed high
with stacks of Exxon floormats
mysteriously stenciled with his name,
rain-rotted sheetrock or miles
of misfitted pipes, coil after coil
of rusted fencewire that stained for days
every crease of me, rollicking it all
to the dump where, while he called
every ragman and ravened junkdog by name,
he catpicked the avalanche of trash
and fished some always fixable thing
up from the depths. His endless aimless work

was not work, my father said.
His barklike earthquake curses
were not curses, for he could *goddamn*
a slipped wrench and *shitfuck* a stuck latch,
but one bad word from me
made his whole being
twang like a nail mis-struck. *Ain't no call for that,*
*Son, no call at all.* Slipknot, whatknot,
knot from which no man escapes—
prestoed back to plain old rope;
whipsnake, blacksnake, deep in the wormdirt
worms like the clutch of mud:
I wanted to live forever
five houses down
in the womanless rooms a woman
sometimes seemed to move through, leaving him
twisting a hand-stitched dishtowel
or idly wiping the volcanic dust.
It was heaven to me:
beans and weenies from paper plates,
black-fingered tinkerings on the back stoop
as the sun set, on an upturned fruitcrate
a little jamjar of rye like ancient light,
from which, once, I took a single, secret sip,
my eyes tearing and my throat on fire.

# TO GRASP AT THE MERCURY MINNOWS ARE

To grasp at the mercury minnows are
or were

in childhood's kingdom
lord of boredom

is to see
through an intimate, ultimate clarity

that galaxy shatter
and like a mind of matter

resolve itself star by slow star.
To grasp at the mercury minnows are . . .

# SITTING DOWN TO BREAKFAST ALONE

*Brachest*, she called it, gentling grease
over blanching yolks with an expertise
honed from three decades of dawns
at the Longhorn Diner in Loraine,
where even the oldest in the old men's booth
swore as if it were scripture truth
they'd never had a breakfast better,
rapping a glass sharply to get her
attention when it went sorrowing
so far into some simple thing—
the jangly door or a crusted pan,
the wall clock's black, hitchy hands—
that she would startle, blink, then grin
as if discovering them all again.
Who remembers now when one died
the space that he had occupied
went unfilled for a day, then two, three,
until she unceremoniously
plunked plates down in the wrong places
and stared their wronged faces
back to banter she could hardly follow.
Unmarried, childless, homely, "slow,"
she knew coffee cut with chamomile
kept the grocer Paul's ulcer cool,
yarrow in gravy eased the islands
of lesions in Larry Borwick's hands,
and when some nightlong nameless urgency
sent him seeking human company

Brother Tom needed hash browns with cheese.
She knew to nod at the litany of cities
the big-rig long-haulers bragged her past,
to laugh when the hunters asked
if she'd pray for them or for the quail
they went laughing off to kill,
and then—envisioning one
rising so fast it seemed the sun
tugged at it—to do exactly that.
Who remembers where they all sat:
crook-backed builders, drought-faced farmers,
VF'ers muttering through their wars,
night-shift roughnecks so caked in black
it seemed they made their way back
every morning from the dead.
Who remembers one word they said?
The Longhorn Diner's long torn down,
the gin and feedlots gone, the town
itself now nothing but a name
at which some bored boy has taken aim,
every letter light-pierced and partial.
Sister, Aunt Sissy, Bera Thrailkill,
I picture you one dime-bright dawn
grown even brighter now for being gone
bustling amid the formica and chrome
of that small house we both called home
during the spring that was your last.
All stories stop: once more you're lost
in something I can merely see:
steam spiriting out of black coffee,

the scorched pores of toast, a bowl
of apple butter like edible soil,
bald cloth, knifelight, the lip of a glass,
my plate's gleaming, teeming emptiness.

## ALL GOOD CONDUCTORS

1.
O the screech and heat and hate
we have for each day's commute,

the long wait at the last stop
before we go screaming

underground, while the pigeons
court and shit and rut

insolently on the tracks
because this train is always late,

always aimed at only us,
who when it comes with its

blunt snout, its thousand mouths,
cram and curse and contort

into one creature, all claws and eyes,
tunneling, tunneling, tunneling

toward money.

**2.**

Sometimes a beauty
cools through the doors at Grand,

glides all the untouchable
angles and planes

of herself
to stand among us

like a little skyscraper,
so sheer, so spare,

gazes going all over her
in a craving wincing way

like sun on glass.

3.
There is a dreamer
all good conductors

know to look for
when the last stop is made

and the train is ticking cool,
some lover, loner, or fool

who has lived so hard
he jerks awake

in the graveyard,
where he sees

coming down the aisle
a beam of light

whose end he is,
and what he thinks are chains

becoming keys.

## IT TAKES PARTICULAR CLICKS

Flip-flops, leash-clinks,
spit on the concrete
like a light slap:
our dawn goon
ambles past, flexing
his pit bull. And soft,
and soon, a low burn
lights the flight path
from O'Hare,
slowly the sky
a roaring flue
to heaven
slowly shut.
Here's a curse
for a car door
stuck for the umpteenth
time, here's a rake
for next door's nut
to claw and claw
at nothing. My nature
is to make
of the speedbump
scraping the speeder's
undercarriage,
and the *om*
of traffic, and somewhere
the helicopter
hovering over

snarls—a kind
of clockwork
from which all things
seek release,
but it takes
particular clicks
to pique my poodle's
interest, naming
with her nose's
particular quiver
the unseeable
unsayable
squirrel. Good girl.

# THE MOLE

After love
discovers it,
the little burn
or birthmark
in an odd spot
he can neither see
nor reach; after
the internist's
downturned mouth,
specialists leaning
over him like
diviners, machines
reading his billion
cells; after
the onslaught
of insight, cures
crawling through him
like infestations,
so many surgeries
a wrong move
leaves him leaking
like overripe fruit;
after the mountain
aster and ice
wine, Michigan
football, *Canes
Venatici* and
the Four North

Fracture Zone
shrink to a room
where voices grow
hushed as if
at some holy
place, and even
in the kindest
eye there lurks
the eternity
to which he's been
commended; after
speech, touch,
even the instinct
to eat are gone,
and he has become
nothing but
a collection of quiet
tics and twitches
as if something
wanted out
of his riddled
bones, the carious
maze of his brain;
as the last day
glaciers into his room,
glass and chrome
so infinites-
imally facet-
ed it seems
he lives inside
a diamond, he breaks

into a wide
smile, as if joy
were the animal
in him, blind,
scrabbling, earth-
covered creature
tunneling
up from God
knows where to stand
upright, feasting
on distances, gazing
dead into the sun.

# DARKCHARMS

In the waiting room, alive together, alone together,
bright hives humming inside of us, in spite of us . . .

*

Radiated, palliated, sheened gray like infected meat,
he takes my hand, gratified, mystified, as if we'd met on the moon.

*

Needle of knowledge, needle of nothingness,
grinding through my spine to sip at the marrow of me.

*

To be so touched, so known, so beloved of nothing:
a kind of chewed-tinfoil shiver of the soul.

*

Animate iron, black junk, seared feelerless, up crawls
my cockroach hope, lone survivor of the fire I am.

*

In the world the world's unchanged to all but you:
iodine dawns, abyss of birdsong, a friend's laughter lashes
    invisible whips.

\*

*How* are *you?* Pity soaks the moment like wet bread.
Do I spit it out, or must I gum this unguent down?

\*

Philosophy of treatment regimens, scripture of obituaries:
heretic, lunatic, I touch my tumor like a charm.

\*

Prevarications, extenuations, tomorrow's tease of being:
we are what we are only in our last bastions.

\*

And past that?
Now, near me, not me, a girl, shameless, veinless, screams.

God goes, belonging to every riven thing he's made
sing his being simply by being
the thing it is:
stone and tree and sky,
man who sees and sings and wonders why

God goes. Belonging, to every riven thing he's made,
means a storm of peace.
Think of the atoms inside the stone.
Think of the man who sits alone
trying to will himself into the stillness where

God goes belonging. To every riven thing he's made
there is given one shade
shaped exactly to the thing itself:
under the tree a darker tree;
under the man the only man to see

God goes belonging to every riven thing. He's made
the things that bring him near,
made the mind that makes him go.
A part of what man knows,
apart from what man knows,

God goes belonging to every riven thing he's made.

## THIS MIND OF DYING

God let me give you now this mind of dying
fevering me back
into consciousness of all I lack
and of that consciousness becoming proud:

>	*There are keener griefs than God.*
>	*They come quietly, and in plain daylight,*
>	*leaving us with nothing, and the means to feel it.*

My God my grief forgive my grief tamed in language
to a fear that I can bear.
Make of my anguish
more than I can make. Lord, hear my prayer.

# ONE TIME

## 1. CANYON DE CHELLY, ARIZONA

Then I looked down into the lovely cut
of a missing river, something under
dusk's upflooding shadows
claiming for itself a clarity
of which my eyes were not yet capable:
fissures could be footpaths, ancient homes
random erosions; pictographs depicting fealties
of who knows what hearts, to who knows what gods.
To believe is to believe you have been torn
from the abyss, yet stand waveringly on its rim.
I come back to the world. I come back
to the world and would speak of it plainly,
with only so much artifice as words
themselves require, only so much distance
as my own eyes impose
on the slickrock whorls of the real
canyon, the yucca's stricken
clench, and, on the other side,
the dozen buzzards swirled and buoyed
above some terrible intangible fire
that must scald the very heart
of matter to cast up such avid ash.

## 2. 2047 GRACE STREET

But the world is more often refuge
than evidence, comfort and covert
for the flinching will, rather than the sharp
particulate instants through which God's being burns
into ours. I say God and mean more
than the bright abyss that opens in that word.
I say world and mean less
than the abstract oblivion of atoms
out of which every intact thing emerges,
into which every intact thing finally goes.
I do not know how to come closer to God
except by standing where a world is ending
for one man. It is still dark,
and for an hour I have listened
to the breathing of the woman I love beyond
my ability to love. Praise to the pain
scalding us toward each other, the grief
beyond which, please God, she will live
and thrive. And praise to the light that is not
yet, the dawn in which one bird believes,
crying not as if there had been no night
but as if there were no night in which it had not been.

## FROM A WINDOW

Incurable and unbelieving
in any truth but the truth of grieving,

I saw a tree inside a tree
rise kaleidoscopically

as if the leaves had livelier ghosts.
I pressed my face as close

to the pane as I could get
to watch that fitful, fluent spirit

that seemed a single being undefined
or countless beings of one mind

haul its strange cohesion
beyond the limits of my vision

over the house heavenwards.
Of course I knew those leaves were birds.

Of course that old tree stood
exactly as it had and would

(but why should it seem fuller now?)
and though a man's mind might endow

even a tree with some excess
of life to which a man seems witness,

that life is not the life of men.
And that is where the joy came in.

## VOICE OF ONE HEAD

They were good times, the end times
(as the preacher called them)
when there was no remoteness that was not wired,
it was possible to live entirely inside,
and every ozone sundown burned a braver creation.

That was the summer when the year was summer.
Smokestacks curlicued their smog
in almost animal shapes,
and the whole nation came together
to watch the two-headed infant speak its first word
on TV.

We were at the edge: I remember music
comprised entirely of surgical sounds;
a daylong documentary
in which a glacier made a lace of ice so fine
the contemplation of that loss
isolated and annihilated time
like a mystic discipline.

True, there were wars,
and true, in some sense they were ours.
But rage was . . . all the rage—
a dinner-party flinch and grimace
by which the like-minded linked (and liked) their minds.

It made little sense to love, but love we did,
flinging ourselves out of ourselves like a river
striking rock
—suspended upended bits of light
grown gloriously plural—
before the tug and the rush and the roar of us onward.

Of course there were things we had to let go.
The fish in the harbor, kaleidoscopic even at night,
floated like rotting rainbows as they died.

Of course there were those whom pills could no longer lift,
with their novels and their pillows,
as if a mildest light were eating them.

And the sandwich boards selling salvation.
And the engine-eyed atheists screaming reason.

Even the preacher, like a private winter, whitened, and
     quietened,
then one Sunday instead of speaking
burned his sermon
so that, he whispered over the ashes after,
there might be finally one fire our eyes would see.

And indeed that day did feel different.
It seemed there was not one of us
not one of us.
Peace rumored through our screens like a breeze.
The sun itself had the shy, pain-shined air of a survivor.
Even the ocean, it was said, was open.

That evening when the sky like a brandied mind
seemed to dream us at our windows
we met each other's eyes and shook our heads
as if we couldn't believe
what we had been given, how beautiful it had been,
and indeed still was,
slurring such last extravagant streaks of light
over the endless city.

## LATE FRAGMENT

How to say this—
my silences were not always mine:
scrabbled hole and the black beyond;
vaporous pond
as if water wanted out of itself;
tip of the sycamore's weird bare reach:
some latency in things leading not so much to speech
as to a halting, haunted art
wherein to master was to miss—
*how to say this, how to say this . . .*

My father was a boatbuilder.
Prow of a man, his world a sea to cleave.
I learned a dangerous patience,
to navigate night, live on nothing, leave.
And my mother, her furious smallness,
her way of saying her blade, the oil and onion's hiss:
from her I learned what lies beneath.

Mystic, Istanbul, Jakarta, Dar es Salaam—
what was I meant to keep?
If the distances to which I've been given
suggest some wantless heaven
of the mind, what in me still traces
the creekbed creases
in the rough skin of the palm
of one so long asleep?

If I say I loved the seagull
tethered to its cry, the cypress's imprisoned winds,
speak to the brink of my hands
a moss-covered rock
soft and knobby as a kitten's skull.
If I say I loved.

Boston, Lisbon, Cardiff, Asunción:
what name is not a horizon?
Somewhere it is evening,
light grown mild and pliable,
wielded by wave and rock,
in the shore's trees torn apart.

## HERMITAGE

What grew there grew in tangled
ways, minor thrivings of thorntrees, shocked
cacti, tumbleweeds maddening
past in the cages of themselves, everywhere a sense of
sharpness and thwartedness, he the last
twisted try of it all. Light meant
work. He honed
a little horizon of iron and dawn,
bowed all day over acres of adamant
flint as if he were sowing sparks. He found
shells brittling back toward their sea,
leaves and twigs more sun
than themselves, and a thousand other fragments
eternity was tugging at,
and wrought it all into a tenuous, tenacious form
as if he were founding ruins—
a man who himself seemed half born,
half hewn, his skin mapped
with damage, sweat slicking the juts and
cliffs of flesh, eyes so like the sky
he seemed at once all-seeing and all skull.
What did he ask of us, who did not once
acknowledge us, came not once among us,
though we woke to footprints
scalding our lawns, a leprosy
of emptiness gone through all our goods?
What covenant did he keep or rage
to break, his shadow flickering

ceaselessly beside him and the distance stricken
with waves as if some bell of being itself
had sounded? He struck
rock and the rootless dust down to a clay that gave
and gave until he was altogether
underground, smoldering
into sleep, worms of dreams
working under his brow. He climbed
to the only rise there was, the cleft
of rock where the huge beehive hung
like nature's brain, suffering himself
to taste its sweetness. He wrung
from time a time to vanish
back into the sheer
shells and the strict mesquites, the heat-cracked
creekbed and the needless weeds, leaving us
to sift the glorious
ash of his existence, like a burned sermon.

# NOT ALTOGETHER GONE

## I. DIPPED INTO FRENZY

Dipped into frenzy
             like a tonged lobster
he squeaked a bit
then stopped

Overnight
             his hair went white

Clean-suited
in a rocking chair
that never rocked
             with a smile
that either included or excluded
utterly

he was every kind of crying
but the kind that you can see

## 2. NOT ALTOGETHER GONE

Not altogether gone
his antic frantic penny-ante-Ahab stabs of madness

honeybunching the stewardess, teasing a little pile
of eyebrows on his tray-table like impossible pixie sticks

swiveling to give the loud grout rep what for
two cloudminded miles over Iowa

then subsiding spastically back
into his particular contortion of quiet

frieze-faced, mouth an unhappened howl, one arm
half-raised half-childlike as if to ask or answer . . .

before he's seized again with a sharp impersonal turbulence
like angry laundry

## 3. FUCK DOMINOES

"I'll follow your toenails
into any hell that you propose
so deeply do they mean your feet
so purely is their pink my soul's

Teach me to polka my walker
to hum dementia's tune
and I'll don diapers with a kinky gleam
slurp stewed prunes with oyster joy

O my pretties cantankered into twisty things
my lonesome irksome debutantes of death
I'll be the girling dervish of Royal Estates
your bug-eyed undruggable, your ear-hair boy"

## 4. AMERICAN CHEESE

To live amid the jackal looks of unlove,
all the relatives circling eerily warily the scent
of their own blood.
                    Some want money, some seek
only peace, but to you the teeth gleam with the same
obscene rapacity.
                    So you rouse yourself
of an afternoon, not leaving your lair
so much as carrying it with you, that moist, almost visible
nimbus of pain, urine, cold coffee, and cable news
crackling occasionally through the stale cloud of it all—

for an outing! a bit of nature, a refreshing stagger
through the fluorescent plains of Walmart:

demons inked on arms, nicotine tans, hoosegow gazes,
chemical grins, galactic buttocks, some terrycloth termagant
shrilling at her overblooded underminded whelp
*Slim! That boy. Goddammit Slim. Slim!*

Welcome to the hell of having everything:
one repentant politician on sixty screens,
van-sized vats of crabgrass toxin,
a solid quarter mile of disposable diapers:
all our impossibles pluraled.

Would Daddy like some rectal gel?
Would Daddy like some single-use oral swabs?
Would Daddy like some Clonezapam Hydrocodone Lyrica
   Trazodone Cymbalta Wellbutrin Lipitor Vesicare?

Yes, Daddy would.

And Daddy would like to go home, too,
you say without saying a word, minding
your invisible balance beam through the unfuturistic
suck-sound of the doors into the incinerator summer
even locusts have brains enough
to stay out of—
                    everywhere abandoned
carts, triceratops-looking trucks, mother upon mother
with a hungry aboriginal howl
coming not quite from her—
                              while beside you
some dropsical shambles of humanity
who could be your grandson or your grandfather
slimes his sluglike fingers into your own
to press a little *God Is Love* medallion still sticky
from its Cracker Jack box—

though, come to think of it, you'd never find such a thing there,
would you?

As in a freak nook of cliff
it would take a lonely soul to descend and see
a kinked tree grows a moment
still as the rock in which it's rooted—
I saw through his wildtime the childtime smile.

**6. NOW, WHEN THERE IS NO NOW TO BURN**

Now, when there is no now to burn,
and those who, despite you, loved you, turn
back to their lives and the fact of your absence
the strangeness is how little strangeness there is
in the blank day, the meaningless depletion, the grief.
It was always all aftermath, your life.

## AND I SAID TO MY SOUL, BE LOUD

Madden me back to an afternoon
I carry in me
not like a wound
but like a will against a wound

Give me again enough man
to be the child
choosing my own annihilations

To make of this severed limb
a wand to conjure
a weapon to shatter
dark matter of the dirt daubers' nests
galaxies of glass

Whacking glints
bash-dancing on the cellar's fire
I am the sound the sun would make
if the sun could make a sound
and the gasp of rot
stabbed from the compost's lumpen living death
is me

O my life my war in a jar
I shake you and shake you
and may the best ant win

For I am come a whirlwind of wasted things
and I will ride this tantrum back to God

until my fixed self, my fluorescent self
my grief-nibbling, unbewildered, wall-to-wall self
withers in me like a salted slug

## HAMMER IS THE PRAYER

*There is no consolation in the thought of God,*
he said, slamming another nail

in another house another havoc had half-taken.
*Grace is not consciousness, nor is it beyond.*

*To hell with remembrance, to hell with heaven,*
*hammer is the prayer of the poor and the dying.*

And as wind in some lordless random comes to rest,
and all the disquieted dust within,

peace came to the hinterlands of our minds,
too remote to know, but peace nonetheless.

## WHEN THE TIME'S TOXINS

When the time's toxins
have seeped into every cell

and like a salted plot
from which all rain, all green, are gone

I and life are leached
of meaning

somehow a seed
of belief

sprouts the instant
I acknowledge it:

little weedy hardy would-be
greenness

tugged upward
by light

while deep within
roots like talons

are taking hold again
of this our only earth.

## SMALL PRAYER IN A HARD WIND

As through a long-abandoned half-standing house
only someone lost could find,

which, with its paneless windows and sagging crossbeams,
its hundred crevices in which a hundred creatures hoard and nest,

seems both ghost of the life that happened there
and living spirit of this wasted place,

wind seeks and sings every wound in the wood
that is open enough to receive it,

shatter me God into my thousand sounds.

FOR D.


Groans going all the way up a young tree
half-cracked and caught in the crook of another

pause. All around the hill-ringed, heavened pond
leaves shush themselves like an audience.

A cellular stillness, as of some huge attention
bearing down. May I hold your hand?

A clutch of mayflies banqueting on oblivion
writhes above the water like visible light.

## LORD IS NOT A WORD

Lord is not a word.
Song is not a salve.
Suffer the child, who lived
on sunlight and solitude.
Savor the man, craving
earth like an aftertaste.
To discover in one's hand
two local stones the size
of a dead man's eyes
saves no one, but to fling them
with a grace you did not know
you knew, to bring them
skimming homing
over blue, is to discover
the river from which they came.
Mild merciful amnesia
through which I've moved
as through a blue atmosphere
of almost and was,
how is it now,
like ruins unearthed by ruin,
my childhood should rise?
Lord, suffer me to sing
these wounds by which I am made
and marred, savor this creature
whose aloneness you ease and are.

## GIVEN A GOD MORE PLAYFUL

Given a god more playful
more sayful
            less prone
to unreachable peaks
and silence at the heart
of stone

I might have plundered
thunder
          from a tick's back

I might have swigged
existence
            from a tulip's bell

and given all hell
to a god who given time

knew goddamn well
what to do with it:

make, and proliferate,
and vanish
              when you are through with it

# IT IS GOOD TO SIT EVEN A ROTTING BODY

*for W. S. Di Piero*

It is good to sit even a rotting body
in sunlight uncompromised
by God, or lack of God,

to see the bee beyond
all the plundered flowers
air-stagger toward you

and like a delicate helicopter
hover above your knee
until it finds you to be

not sweet but at least
not flinching, its hair-legs
on the hair of your leg

silvering
a coolness through you
like a soul of nerve.

# GONE FOR THE DAY, SHE IS THE DAY

Dawn is a dog's yawn, space
in bed where a body should be,
a nectared yard, night surviving
in wires through which what voices,
what needs already move—and the mind
nibbling, nibbling at Nothingness
like a mouse at cheese:

Spring!

*


Sometimes one has the sense
that to say the name
God is a great betrayal,
but whether one is betraying
God, language, or one's self
is harder to say.

*


Gone for the day, she is the day
opening in and around me
like flowers she planted in our yard.
Christ. Not flowers.
Gone for the day, she is the day
razoring in with the Serbian roofers,
and ten o'clock tapped exactly

by the one bad wheel of the tortilla cart,
and the newborn's noonday anguish
eased. And the *om* the mind
makes of traffic and the bite
of reality that brings it back.
And the late afternoon afterlight
in which a much-loved dog lies
like a piece of precocious darkness
lifting his ears at threats, treats, comings, goings . . .

\*

To love is to feel your death
given to you like a sentence,
to meet the judge's eyes
as if there were a judge,
as if he had eyes,
and love.

# STOLEN AIR

*Selected Poems of*

*Osip Mandelstam*

In 2013 I published a short selection of "translations" of Osip Mandelstam's poetry. The word is in quotes because, as I wrote in an afterword, the book actually contained three types of poems: traditional translations faithful to the originals, freer hybrid forms that were really "versions," and then a few wild visions of/collisions with Mandelstam that I didn't really know how to name. The poems that follow are all from this last category. The one exception is "Black Candle," which is a straightforward translation, and which I include because it remains one of my favorites.

## CATHEDRAL, EMPTY

When light, failing,
Falling

Through stained glass,
Liquefies

The long grass
At the feet of Christ,

I crawl diabolical
To the foot of the cross

To sip the infinite
Tenderness

Distilled
From destroyed

Hearts:
An air of thriving

Hopelessness
Like a lone cypress

Holding on
To some airless

Annihilating height.

## NOT ONE WORD

Not one word.
Purge the mind of what the eye has seen:
Woman, prison, bird.
Everything.

Otherwise some wrong dawn
Your mouth moves
And a sudden pine
Needles through your nerves,

A trapped wasp crazes
In your brain,
And in the old desk's ink stain
A forest mazes

Inward and inward
To the unpicked
And sun-perfected
Blueberries

Where you now and now always
Must stand,
An infinite inch
Between that sweetness

And your hand.

# NIGHT PIECE

Come love let us sit together
In the cramped kitchen breathing kerosene.
There's fuel enough to forget the weather,
The knife is ours and the bread is clean.

Come love let us play the game
Of what to take and when to run,
Of come with me and come what may
And holding hands to hold off the sun.

# HERZOVERSE

Once upon a time there lived a Jew,
A musical Jew, I tell you,
Named Alexander Herzowitz.
Sweet as sherbet, his Schubert,
A jewel, I tell you, a musical jewel,

Dawn to dusk, day after day,
The same damn jewel in the same damn way:
What is this, Salamander Slivovitz,
Insanity's sonata?
And what are you, a holy fool?

Scherzowitz! Enoughofits!
Let the *dulce de leche* maiden
Swoon Schubert through her skin,
Let the children's sleigh allegro
This swiftness and darkness and starsparkle snow.

We're not afraid to die,
You and I,
To flutter down like a dove, a musical dove,
To hang on a black hook like a coat and glove,
A worn, one-armed coat and a tattered, three-fingered glove.

O maestro, Alexander Herzowitz,
Whose hands and heart are blown to bits,
What in you pins you there,
My lonely mister, heaven's busker,
Playing your sad, your same, your only air?

Fuck this sulk, these pansy stanzas tickling doom.
Devil me down to the roots of my hair,
And further—ah, François, *le barbier débonnaire*,
Scalp me back to the Paris of youth!

Odds are I'm alive.
Odds are, like a jockey gone to slop,
There's skip and nimble in me yet,
There's a length of neck to stake, and there's cunning,
And there's an animal under me running
Which, if I can hold on, will not stop.

Thirty-one years alive in cherry white,
Thirty-one years belong to blossoms.
Who hears them, the earthworms like jellied rain
Chewing through soil and the solid dead
While all of tall-sailed Moscow whips and snaps
In the instant's wind?

Easy, boy: impatience, too, is candy,
And we are sulk-soft, silk-kneed, mild.
Let's take the track early, and pace ourselves,
Until all the trapped acids trickle out as sweat,
And we take time between our teeth like a bit
And let fly the wild.

Like water trickling from the highest ice
Its bracing ache, its brain-shard sweetness,
Its nowhere air of utter now,

So my sigh has lost its source,
And I live by meanings I cannot comprehend,
For every instant I must taste the instant that I end.

## BLACK CANDLE

Your girlish shoulders are for blushing,
For blushing under whips, and in dawn's raw ice to shine.

Your childlike hands are for pushing,
For pushing flatirons and feed sacks, and knotting twine.

Your feet, infant-tender, are for tiptoeing,
Tiptoeing through shattered glass, in the blood-tracked clay.

And I, I am for you, a black candle burning,
Like a black candle I am burning, and dare not pray.

## STEPPES

Openness or emptiness, I'm sick of it:
Horizon everywhere,
Infinity forced down the gullet:
Eat your god, child, and love it!
To be blinded would be a mercy here.

Better to live alluvial,
Better to live layered downward,
To be a man of sand, of hollows, shallows,
To cling to sleeves of water
And to let them go—

An eon's tune, an instant's.
I might have rained the rapids back.
I might have learned to hear
In any random rotting log
A tree release its rings year by slow year.

## SORROWDRAWL

Shut up: to be alone is to be alive,
To be alive to be a man—
Even hazied, even queasied by this madsmash hinterland,
Lost and locked in the sky's asylum eye.

This is my prayer to the air
To which I turn and turn expecting news or ease,
Nerves minnowing from shadowhands
Toward shadowlands inside of me. This is my prayer

To be of and under a human-scale sky,
To suffer a human-scale why, to leave
This blunt sun, these eternal furrows,
For the one country that comes when I close my eyes.

# FAITH

To taste in each leaf's sticky oath
The broken promise that is earth.

Mother of maple, mother of snow,
See how strong, how blind I grow,
Obeying rain, intuiting roots . . .

Frogs, all ooze and noise, bellvowel
Their bodies into a single aural oil.

Are these my eyes erupting green?
This my mouth mist seeks to mean?

Mother of maple, mother of snow . . .

And I was alive in the blizzard of the blossoming pear,
Myself I stood in the storm of the bird-cherry tree.
It was all leaflife and starshower, unerring, self-shattering power,
And it was all aimed at me.

What is this dire delight flowering fleeing always earth?
What is being? What is truth?

Blossoms rupture and rapture the air,
All hover and hammer,
Time intensified and time intolerable, sweetness raveling rot.
It is now. It is not.

FROM

ONCE
IN THE
WEST

## PRAYER

For all
the pain

passed down
the genes

or latent
in the very grain

of being;
for the lordless

mornings,
the smear

of spirit
words intuit

and inter;
for all

the nightfall
neverness

inking
into me

even now,
my prayer

is that a mind
blurred

by anxiety
or despair

might find
here

a trace
of peace.

*from*

_____

# SUNGONE
# NOON

## BACK

Goof the noon
no one knows

back of the house
back of the shed

back of God
with his everair

assurances
and iron

injunctions:
sing a little nonce

curse
for the curse

of consciousness
coming on you

like a rash:
little boy

lifting
little mountains

from the trash
to stare down

the angry
eons

in the oil eyes
of the horny toad.

Goof the noon
gone too soon

like the house
and shed,

like the boy
in whom you sit,

your back
to the back

of the old
commode,

where a few flowers
flower

out of all the years
of shit.

NATIVE

At sixteen,
sixteen miles

from Abilene
(Trent,

to be exact),
hellbent

on being not
this, not that,

I drove
a steamroller

smack-dab over
a fat black snake.

Up surged a cheer
from men

so cheerless
cheers

were grunts, squints,
whisker twitches

it would take
a lunatic acuity

to see.
I saw

the fat black snake
smashed flat

as the asphalt
flattening

under all ten tons
of me,

flat as the landscape
I could see

no end of,
flat as the affect

of distant killing
vigilance

it would take a native
to know was love.

## KEYNOTE

I had a dream of Elks,
antlerless but arousable all the same,

before whom I proclaimed the Void
and its paradoxical intoxicating joy,

infinities of fields our very natures
commanded us to cross,

the Sisyphean satisfaction of a landscape
adequate to loss—

and as I spoke inspired
farther and farther afield from my notes

I saw James Wesson whiten
to intact ash

big-boned Joe Sloane shrivelcrippled
tight as tumbleweed

I saw wren-souled Mary Flynn die again
in Buzz's eyes

I saw
I saw

like a huge claw
time tear

through the iron
armory and the baseball fields

the slush-puppy stand
the little pier at Towle Park Pond

until I stood strangered
before the living staring Godfearing men

who knew me when.

# RUST

*Mamie Thrailkill, 1894–1990*

A hammer a father's forever behind
or a Dust Bowl woodpecker high in pines?

Blue purl and milkfeel of a child taking shape,
or child-sized tumor taking over?

She sits in the timestorm time's turned into,
shinedying in her easy chair.

Love is there:

handmade houseshoes and a cairn of yarn;
a Bible thumbed to nearly nothing;

the percolator's way of holding and withholding
every inmost stare and state.

And hate:

purple-kerchiefed, stupid-toothed, a Stuckey's Aunt Jemima
stalls her grin above a red cut of melon;

on the sideboard a lean late husband
hatchets through a half-dozen grainy days.

Shy birdbride, fourteen, all night you hide
under the bed divining sighs, each

                      iron
                            squeak.


Sweet Christ! how much itch and last sass
must a middle-aged man with one mean mule


and a patch of pissed-on dirt endure?
Not much, not much.


Is nothing pure?
Is it the soul's treason to think so?


Is it nature's to wink so
on the birdhouse hinges and the chain-links


until the brain breaks
upon a paingleaned God


too meaningful
to mean?


*I just went to bed*, she said
of her son's sons' deaths just days apart


from slapcheek,
from brain fever,


from the virus
of us.

And art?

When the rocking stops.
A sense of being henceforth always after.

A hungry angry mule crying its dumb ton
of rust.

## WE LIVED

We lived in the long intolerable called God.
We seemed happy.

I don't mean content I mean heroin happy,
donkey dentures,

I mean drycleaned deacons expunging suffering
from Calcutta with the cut of their jaws

I mean the always alto and surely anusless angels
divvying up the deviled eggs and jello salad in the after-rapture

I mean
to be mean.

Dear Lord forgive the love I have
for you and your fervent servants.

I have so long sojourned Lord
among the mild ironies and tolerable gods

that what comes first to mind
when I'm of a mind to witness

is muriatic acid
eating through the veins

of one whose pains were so great
she wanted only out, Lord, out.

She too worshipped you.
She too popped her little pill of soul.

Lord if I implore you please just please leave me alone
is that a prayer that's every instant answered?

I remember one Wednesday witness told of a time
his smack-freaked friends lashed him

to the back of a Brahman bull that bucked and shook
until like great bleeding wings the man's collarbones

exploded out of his skin.
Long pause.

"It was then," the man said, "right *then* . . ."
Yes. And how long before that man-

turned-deacon-turned-scourge-of-sin
began his ruinous and (one would guess) Holy Spirit–less affair?

At what point did this poem abandon
even the pretense of prayer?

Imagine a man alive in the long intolerable time
made of nothing but rut and rot,

a wormward gaze
even to his days' sudden heavens.

There is the suffering existence answers:
it carves from cheeks and choices the faces

we in fact are;
and there is the suffering of primal silence,

which seeps and drifts like a long fog
that when it lifts

leaves nothing
but the same poor sod.

Dear God—

## SUNDAY SCHOOL

A city of loss lit in me.

Childhood: all the good
Godcoddled children

chiming past
the valley of the shadow:

old pews, old views
of the cotton fields

north, south,
east, west,

foreverness
sifting down like dust

when—

        stabdazzling darkness,
        icequiet:

        towers of glare,
        blacksleek streets,

        everywhere an iron
        eloquence

and a sense
of high finish

hived with space
like a face

honed
by a loneliness

it never came
to know.

I came to know it.

## MEMORY'S MERCIES

Memory's mercies
mostly aren't

but there were
I swear
            days
veined with grace

like a lucky
rock
            ripping
electrically over

whatever water
there was—

ten skips
            twenty
in the telling:

all the day's aches
eclipsed

and a late sun
belling

even sleeping Leroy
back
          into his body
to smile
at some spirit-lit

tank-rock
skimming the real

so belongingly
no longing
              clung to it
when it plunged

bright as a firefly
into nowhere,

I swear.

# BELIEVING GREEN

*2810 El Paso Street, 1974*

Solitary as a mast on a mountaintop,
an ocean of knowing long withdrawn,

she dittied the days, grew fluent in cat,
felt, she said, each seed surreptitiously split

the adamantine dark, believing green.
It was the town's torpor washed me to her door,

it was the itch existence stranded me on that shore
of big-lipped shells pinked with altogether other suns,

random wall-blobs impastoed with jewels and jowls
sometimes a citizen seemed to peek through,

inward and inward all the space and spice
of her edible heavens.

O to feel again within the molded dough
wet pottery, buttery cosmos, brain that has not cooled;

to bring to being an instant
sculpture garden: five flashlit jackrabbits locked in black.

From her I learned the earthworm's exemplary open-mindedness,
its engine of discriminate shit.

From her I learned all the nuances of neverness
that link the gladiola to God.

How gone she must be, graveless maybe,
who felt the best death would be for friends to eat you,

whose last name I never even knew:
dirt-rich mouse-proud lady who Rubied me

into a life so starred and laughtered there was no need
for after.

## LOVE'S LAST

Love's last urgency is earth
and grief is all gravity

and the long fall always
back to earliest hours

that exist nowhere
but in one's brain.

From the hard-packed
pile of old-mown grass,

from boredom, from pain,
a boy's random slash

unlocks a dark ardor
of angry bees

that link the trees
and block his way home.

I like to hold him holding me,
mystery mastering fear,

so young, standing unstung
under what survives of sky.

I learned too late how to live.
Child, teach me how to die.

*from*

_____

# MY STOP
# IS GRAND

## MY STOP IS GRAND

I have no illusion
some fusion
      of force and form
will save me,
bewilderment
      of bonelight
ungrave me

as when the El
shooting through a hell
      of ratty alleys
where nothing thrives
but soot
      and the ratlike lives
that have learned to eat it

screechingly peacocked
a grace of sparks
      so far out and above
the fast curve that jostled
and fastened us
      into a single shock of—
I will not call it love

but at least some brief
and no doubt illusionary belief
      that in one surge of brain

we were all seeing
one thing:
        a lone unearned loveliness
struck from an iron pain.


Already it was gone.
Already it was bone,
        the gray sky
and the encroaching skyline
pecked so clean
        by raptor night
I shuddered at the cold gleam


we hurtled toward
like some insentient herd
        plunging underground at Clark
and Division.
And yet all that day
        I had a kind of vision
that's never gone completely away


of immense clear-paned towers
and endlessly expendable hours
        through which I walked
teeming human streets,
filled with a shine
        that was most intimately me
and not mine.

## LITTLE KILLING DITTY

I have forgotten the little killing ditty
whispered to the red birds and the blue birds and the brown birds
not one of which I ever thought to give a name.

In the tall mesquite mistaking our yard
for a spacious place, I plugged away with my pellet gun
and got them often even in the eye, for I was trained

to my craft by primordial boredom
and I suppose some generic, genetic rage
I seem to have learned to quell, or kill.

They dropped like the stones I'd throw in Catclaw Creek
or fluttered spastically and panickedly up
whereupon I took more tenacious aim—

much more difficult now because they moved
—not me, frozen as if in a camera's flash—
troubling the tyranny of the ordinary

as if a wave of meaning or unmeaning
went rippling like heat through the yard.
Fire and fire and they fell and they fall, hard.

I felt nothing, and I will not betray those days
if days are capable of being betrayed,
by pretending a pang in my larval heart

or even some starveling joy when Tuffy yelped.
I took aim at the things I could not name.
And the ditty helped.

## THE PREACHER ADDRESSES THE SEMINARIANS

I tell you it's a bitch existence some Sundays
and it's no good pretending you don't have to pretend,

don't have to hitch up those gluefutured nags Hope and Help
and whip the sorry chariot of yourself

toward whatever hell your heaven is on days like these.
I tell you it takes some hunger heaven itself won't slake

to be so twitchingly intent on the pretty organist's pedaling,
so lizardly alert to the curvelessness of her choir robe.

Here it comes, brothers and sisters, the confession of sins,
hominy hominy, dipstick doxology, one more churchcurdled hymn

we don't so much sing as haunt: grounded altos, gear-grinding tenors,
two score and ten gently bewildered men lip-synching along.

You're up, Pastor. Bring on the unthunder. Some trickle-piss tangent
to reality. Some bit of the Gospel grueling out of you.

I tell you sometimes mercy means nothing
but release from this homiletic hologram, a little fleshstep

sideways, as it were, setting passion on autopilot (as if it weren't!)
to gaze out in peace at your peaceless parishioners:

boozeglazes and facelifts, bad mortgages, bored marriages,
a masonry of faces at once specific and generic,

and here and there that rapt famished look that leaps
from person to person, year to year, like a holy flu.

All these little crevices into which you've crawled
like a chubby plumber with useless tools:

Here, have a verse for your wife's death.
Here, have a death for your life's curse.

I tell you some Sundays even the children's sermon
—maybe especially this—sharks your gut

like a bite of tin some beer-guzzling goat
either drunkenly or mistakenly decides to sample.

I know what you're thinking. Christ's in this.
He'll get to it, the old cunner, somewhere somehow

there's the miracle meat, the aurora borealis blood,
every last atom compacted to a grave

and the one thing that every man must lose to save.
Well, friends, I'm here to tell you two things today.

First, though this is not, for me, one of those bilious abrading days,
though in fact I stand before you in a rage of faith

and have all good hope that you will all go help
untold souls back into their bodies,

ease the annihilating No above which they float,
the truth is our only savior is failure.

Which brings me to the second thing: that goat.
It was real. It is, as is usually the case, the displacement of agency

that is the lie. It was long ago, Mexico, my demon days.
It was a wager whose stakes I failed to appreciate.

He tottered. He flowered. He writhed time to a fraught quiet,
and kicked occasionally, and lay there twitching, watching me die.

# WITNESS

Typically cryptic, God said three weasels
slipping electric over the rocks
one current conducting them up the tree
by the river in the woods of the country
into which I walked
away and away and away;
and a moon-blued, cloud-strewn night sky
like an X-ray
with here a mass and there a mass
and everywhere a mass;
and to the tune of a two-year-old
storm of atoms
elliptically, electrically alive—
*I will love you in the summertime, Daddy.*
*I will love you . . . in the summertime.*

Once in the west I lay down dying
to see something other than the dying stars
so singularly clear, so unassailably there,
they made me reach for something other.
I said I will not bow down again
to the numinous ruins.
I said I will not violate my silence with prayer.
I said *Lord, Lord*
in the speechless way of things
that bear years, and hard weather, and witness.

## ANTIQUITY TOO

Antiquity too
had arms, legs, loins,

and while its shadows thrashed on stone
it would one day be,

fucked, flicker-lit, like you, like me.

—*after Goethe*

## AFTER A STORM

My sorrow's flower was so small a joy
It took a winter seeing to see it as such.
Numb, unsteady, stunned at all the evidence
Of winter's blind imperative to destroy,
I looked up, and saw the bare abundance
Of a tree whose every limb was lit and fraught with snow.
What I was seeing then I did not quite know
But knew that one mite more would have been too much.

## VARIETIES OF QUIET

*Varieties*
*of quiet*

I quote
from a poet

no one knows.
And no one

knows
me too

if by chance
happening

here
some far year

when I am
not:

it matters
I tell you

it matters
the matter

one mind
collects,

one memory
protects

when memory's
kin

to that wordless
feeling

words
open in your head:

*varieties*
*of quiet*

*varieties*
*of quiet*

There are many
friend

as many
as the dead.

# MORE LIKE
# THE STARS

I don't want to be alive anymore.
I don't want to be alive enough to want that.

One is not meant to turn on one's creator
with ferocity expendable in only one way.

Or is that exactly how one is meant to turn
to burn

beyond the love that from beyond being
has come to us:

Christ's ever unhearable
and thus always too bearable
scream.

In love and dread we learn to listen
for beloved dread

coming upon us like a whiplash rain
we watch through a window.

In pain we learn pain.

Sometimes amid the rancid moonlight and mindlice of my insomnia
there gleams a scalpel blade

so clean with meaning
so shaped and sharpened to interstellar blue

that drawing it—in season due—
across my own throat

there comes not blood but an ancient answering
starlight.

Once upon a time in a pleasingly modern slaughterhospice
with a view of sky-contempted skyscrapers

and Lake Michigan's immaculate sewage
my inner skin was skinned mouth to bowels,

my soul—deadword, die to find it.

For self-pity there must remain a self.
Ah, but even shitting one's self

one still finds one's self hastening to hide it all
from the kind Ukrainian nearly bearded night nurse.

Fentanyl patches patching my stalactite thighs
my diaphanous shoulders

the very air eating me
like a late leaf

that once I would have flourished
for a perishable lover

or lonelied like some catpiss poignancy
into a poem.

Dead brain, living will, little pills
entangling pain with adoration of it,

morphine machine whose little beep
(heavenly bell)

conjures me to the suddenly more tolerable hallways
of hell . . .
                    Lovely Leila,

so unsurgically curved,
disclosing as she leans to clean my lines

a bit of icelace undergarment like the very last trace
of a glacier.

The brain the brain the brain flickering electrically
in and out,

in,
            out—

not the mind in which I love
my wife

whose tightwound nightmind conjures Christ in diapers,
for instance, filthy infant, or later,

in a mist of adolescent bad weather,
bored of wood, dogdead Judea, squawk-box God,

some restless absurdity of earth, she says,
through which the rest of heaven can come.

Once upon a time I walked through the chemical glamour
of a night refinery

sparking dangerously without and within
for beside me under her underclothes

undulated an incarnation
of creation's finest failure:

moonskin to make a young man wince
coupled with stifling innocence.

Still, we managed.

And over the wrought-iron railing of the country club
to which neither of us could possibly belong,

in the moonskinned pool that seemed both to embody and imbibe
her, we improved.

And later, out on a green (to be sixteen!)
when the starshower I thought was mine

was mining me for sweat, muscle, memory
to make its own death

shine unceasingly inside of me
even unto hell,

                we excelled.

Can it be that her last name was really Key?

So much life in this poem
so much salvageable and saving love

but it is I fear I swear I tear open
what heart I have left

to keep it from being
and beating and bearing down upon me

What rest in faith
wrested
          from grief?

What truce
          with truth
in bowing
down

not to the ground
of being
          but simply
to the ground?

Affliction flickers
distant
          now
like a structure
on fire.
          Love's
reprieve
moves through me

like a breeze

But antlike
          existence
crawls all over me Lord

and I cry out
if you call
            this vise
quiet
            a cry
this riot
of needs and genes
an I

Feelingly
            among the
bones
            and nerves
of sounds
I make my scathing
way
            Failingly
in church
or in the parked
car
            before work
I try
            to pray

What might it mean
to surrender
            to the wonder
nothing
            means

Not to end
        with a little flourish
                of earth

Not to end

Love is the living heart of dread

Love I love you unto the very edge of being

Dead

Something in us suffering touches,
teaches first to find

little coves in our loves: blank nothings
wherein we are what we always were

      —blank nothings—

but changed or rearranged
as atoms
        in the random
            kingdom
                of things:

*hand*, we say, or *eye*, or *hair*,
as if to make ourselves—to stake ourselves—truly
there

Knowing now not to move in time
we are moved
           by tiger-striped tails
bloodfine fins

some natureless cerulean
one would say

thinking oneself
out of nature

Something in us, suffering, touches,
torches,
          so we may saunter
seeingly
through an altogether other

element,
as once in the Shedd Aquarium in Chicago

          I floated          a moment

with my love and the two new lives
borne from us
                    who loved best
the eensy
          green
                    almost
                              unfish

more like the stars

when you close your eyes and whirl
open to the whirling

grains
so freed from things
                    you fall
                              down
                                        laughing
at the havoc

For me for a long time
not the minnows mattered

but the pattern after: miraculous
I didn't think

to think:
all those mite-eyes and animate instants

answering at once to my need
and to nothing

as if my very nerves worked
in finally a saving sense

Something in us touches
suffering
            touching
us

like the constellations
of kinetic quiet

that bound us beyond us
as right to the wall the girls pressed

their still-forming faces
through which the wild new schools flew
                              almost
                    too green
              too blue
        to stand

And I held your hand.

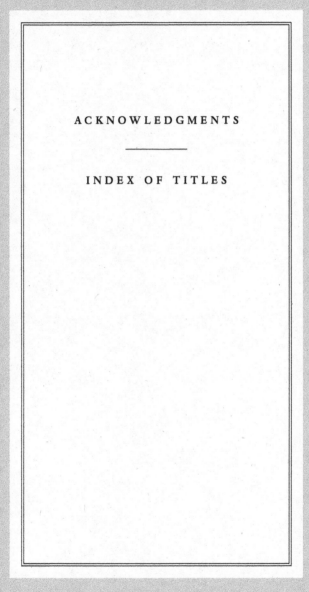

ACKNOWLEDGMENTS

———

INDEX OF TITLES

## ACKNOWLEDGMENTS

Grateful acknowledgment is made to the editors of the following publications, where versions of these poems first appeared: *The American Scholar, The Atlantic Monthly, At Length, Books and Culture, CellPoems, The Christian Century, Commonweal, The Cortland Review, Critical Quarterly, Design Observer, Economy, First Things, Grand Street, Harvard Divinity Bulletin, Heat, The Hopkins Review, Image, Kentucky Poetry Review, The Nation, Negative Capability, The New Criterion, The New England Review, The New Ohio Review, The New Yorker, Occasional Religion, Orion, The Plum Review, Poet & Critic, Poetry, Poetry Daily, Poetry International, Poetry Ireland Review, Poetry Northwest, The Rumpus, The Sewanee Review, Shenandoah, Slate, Southern Review, Spiritus, The Threepenny Review, Tikkun, TriQuarterly,* and *32 Poems.*

I am grateful to Copper Canyon Press for allowing me to reprint the poems from *The Long Home* and *Hard Night.*

I am grateful to Ecco Press for allowing me to reprint the poems from *Stolen Air: Selected Poems of Osip Mandelstam.*

And finally—but firstly!—I'm grateful to Danielle Chapman, Jonathan Galassi, Ilya Kaminsky, and Atsuro Riley for their help with this book.

# INDEX OF TITLES